Judged

©2014 Poetic Minds Publishing LLC

Poetic Minds
Publishing

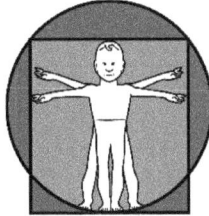

Printed in the U.S.A.

Cover and interior art by Janice Duke
Edition First Printing: March 2014

ISBN: 978-0-9916171-0-4

DEDICATIONS

This book is dedicated to all the people who have inspired the creative journey through the endless never of our poetic endeavors.

TABLE OF CONTENTS

Book of Passion

"Take a Closer Look"

Somewhere, sometime, someone
Will take a closer look
And smile at the sun
Joy will fill empty hearts
As pain is seared away
Light will filter out dark
As long as we stay together and pray
Through rituals and unending night
Powers of perception
Take on a new flight
Swinging from the sky
A saucer full of secrets
Unlocked doors
Leading nowhere and everywhere
To be free and let all see

"Love Angel"

She is a spiral Goddess
Floating in and out of a dream state
Unconscious beauty of sensual taste
Shimmering upon the shore
These images come down from above
Filled with love
May those crystal eyes never tear
Never hold true fear
She has it all at her feet
As she sits upon a queens seat
Sweet undeniable and soft in texture
Has my mind reeling
For a wonderers adventure
Hold true to the love you know
Together let it show
Let it flow
Let her know

"Grace"

Early morning glow
She stirs
Eyes flicker open
Breath caught in my chest
After another night
Soaring with the stars
Swinging on unnatural vines
As they seem to entwine
Our souls and minds
She slowly moves
With the grace only God hands out
I'm entranced and go distant
As my thoughts try to grasp
The enormity of it all
Her eyes align together with mine
Understanding
Desire
Dare I say more

"One Wish"

She's a feather
Floating for forever
The windy weather
Does well to manipulate
This angelic treasure
Bits of her clever wit
And pleasure fix
Lifts me to heights
That don't exist
Only the billowing breeze
Flowing through her sleeves
All the while

Has her gliding on clouds
Above the trees
She's a product of perfect
In any dialect
She's of divinity fate
Simple to sketch
Yet impossible to duplicate
Blow me the kiss
From the heavens
Enter me on the list
For eternal bliss
Lying within a soul
A sanctuary
Impossible to miss

"Body"

As my eyes close
Dreams take over
Eyes reopen
Gazing softly into deep blues
I touch her face with my fingertips
My lips brush her soft and perfect lips
A spark of energy ignites
My body moving and heart racing
Our touches get faster as we explore each other
For the ten thousandth time
It's still all new
And she's the focus of my love rhyme
Her body is perfectly formed
Long legs, slim waist, soft long hair
Full lips, voluptuous breasts
My hands roam all over her
Deep into unknown regions
Our heat flowing and driving me nuts
Together our bodies form one
In love
I'm in love with her
This is her body
Sleek and full of beauty
A tigress in animalistic grace

"Love is a Passing of Time"

Survey the circle of intuitive glances
Draw meaning from the unspoken word
Your mind in disruptive dances
Eyes glace toward the untold
Now left to wonder alone
With a life without a home
Wondering what is real, what can be undone
Until the spark of recognition
Awakens your dead soul
You stir
And a strange feeling washes over you
Your alive and in control
Walking below hand in hand
With the regret of lost time
Wishing upon a star
And writing in cynical rhyme
Walking in suggested circles
For the blind path you're now on
Bewilderment leads you to grasp the unknown
You latch onto love
And die once

"I Wish it Was Scripted"

I close my eyes and drift to bliss
Cascading to my perfect place
Endless green fields, flowing streams
This holy land of dreams
It doesn't seem perfect without you
As the sun crests over the horizon
To the onset of the star gleam
The lightest mist falls from the blessed sky
Giving this mysterious sparkle
To everything the moonlight touches
And just then, my angel appears
Nothing else matters
The stars shed the tears from her eyes
And her essence flatters even the night skies
This princess turned queen
Has me feel peaceful and serene
And has only grown more beautiful
Over the years
As I awake
I know only time will tell
What looms ahead
If this will spell doom
Or love instead

"Windswept Muse"

Another escapade
Another face invades
Finds the path to my heart cage
Divides what remains
The hourglass of time
Has run bone dry
Her mystery is without rhyme
With the farewell kiss goodbye
Her fragrance was wine
Surrounded by a rampant beast
Who wants her to die
By pains insistent beat
I stand in the darkened alcove
Once again tasting beauty
That could have been love
Reality blossoms from the tip of the cigarette
And I think to the above
How many tests
Do I have to forget

"Panacea"

Inspiration comes in doses
Like stumbling into the desert
And finding a bright patch of roses
Like catching a glimpse of the sun
Before a thunderstorm approaches
It could come as drastic as this
Or just the right words
That drives you to a moment of bliss
For me, it's all about mood
Getting caught in a movie
Or playing that rhythm that so eludes
Even still, fighting away
Memories of gray
And overcoming something
Or even to pray
For anything to be a better way
All this salivates in my brain
Coming finally together
From feelings to words
And here forever
To this, a picture perfect place
Of my panacea

"Succumb to Love"

Turn the page
To different views
Only so far
Locked in my cage
I wonder 5 steps and stop
Turn and ponder the path
I stop and watch
Turn 5 steps and stop
The great wide open
Greets me with possibilities
Shares with me
Takes from me
Spins me into the future
Gaze deep with eyes wide
Stare with head high
To your unending sky
Relive your pain and lies
Learn from your time
So the cage will crumble

"Silk Prose"

The poetry I spit is sultry
Slowly flowing forth with ease
Writing poems under this oak tree
Rhymes tantalizing in the breeze
The creek bed nearby
Eases my worried mind
As the words I speak
Never cease to bring me to peace
Sipping on this heavenly champaign
Dancing in this real rain
Growing from the knowledge of true gain
Hoping to never lose my eye sparkle
From hellish pain

"Jump Start"

Those eyes hold my love
Deepness and vastness
Endless love
This goes far beyond
Your features
This goes far beyond
Your softness
This reaches deeper into the unknown
To a place of peace
I can call home
How long have I awaited
This powerful feeling
A rising from a dead heart
She is like a jump start
That never flames out
A force beyond the light
Something so wonderful
It's hard to put into words
Hard to put into action
All I can say is that
The love I have
Is as true as it gets

"Higher Love"

I sense a sequence
The portrait of love
Variables blend to their patterns
As seen by the God above
Induces a strength
Born over the years
As friendship has its bond
That grows with tears
Whatever comes along
The pain and misfortune
She's still there, by my side
As we continue
On a wild love ride
Sometimes I look to the sky
Not to wonder why
As advice screams down from all around
What I know is right doesn't come from a crowd
It's the connection
God gave me
To this wonderful world of creation
As only together we can be

"Spiral Avenues"

Down spiral avenues
Separation gives way
Love ensues
Parts the seas waves
Running through this kingdom
Powered by her touch
She is freedom
Carrying my torch
Love in eyes of azure
Feeling her soul
As the statues are moving
Will the Gods let me go
Give me my self-control
Sear away my ego
Protect me with strength
Let me know without question
Free of this detention and segregation
Let this be enacted

"First Love"

Come earth Goddess
Shower me with your divinity
Open my doors to infinity
You've captured me in your glow
Drown me in the current flow
Now every face reflects yours
From the high skies to the sandy shores
I'm caged in love
That can never be
Chained from above
Never to be free
Of course I can't be mad
You showed me love
When times we're bad
You let me see inside you
Inside your mind and heart
So now I'm left just to dream
To float in the current of your stream
I'll never forget
And I don't regret
Anything about the first
And only love I'll ever have

"Nothing Left Unsaid"

Running in circles
Blinded by loves cycles
Tripping over swirling feelings
Tight of chest
Short of words
Hand to breast
Love untold
Whispered nothings
Meaning the world
Linger on lips
Frozen drawl
Haunted he runs
To the depths of disparity
Alone and undone
He has no clarity
He waited too long
She waited so long
For so too long
Loves simple words were waiting

"Entranced in a Single Hair"

Caught in her radiant light
Seen in the darkest of nights
Wakes of feeling waves
Can't decide caught in a daze
Her golden blonde hair
Done with her special care
Her beautiful face
Is something that can never be replaced
Her bright shining eyes
Hides her unknown inner cries
Icy tears roll down her cheeks
Her pain is felt for weeks
She seems me there, stare
Our eyes meet with a glare
I look the other way
How could I take my eyes away

Drawn to my knees
Her power exceeds
By her fiery eyes
Glowing in the night skies
Slowly stroking her hair
Enveloped in her lair
Sweet whispers in her ear
Entwined with this new fear
Where is she from
What have I become
Her beauty is a star
Pictured from afar
My minds great flights
Working to overwhelming heights
Grazing over the fire
Flooded with wanting desire

"Trailing the Walls"

Blinking lights
Flicker and fade
Delightful insights
Rolling downward
He alone sees
He alone glows
He alone shows
He alone knows
A gentle touch
Loves brush
A smile
A blush
A sentimental rush
Behold the truth
You dreamed in youth
You will never remove

This love root
I walk eyes half closed
Down the dark hall
Your naked and exposed fingers
Trailing the walls
Your head held high
Your eyes lit like the morning sky
Your soul aglow
In the love you show
We touch moonlights below
As we rest upon her in flow
Gliding past gliding light
Sending us special sight
To light the darkest night
We entwine within this height
You know your name
We are the same
We are the perfect team

"Timeless"

Do you hear the sound of my heartbeat
Do you listen as the heat seeps from the empty side
of the bed sheet
Would you move to stop me before I disappear
Or would your stay frozen in fear
As your lone tear crystalizes
Marking the end of another forgetful year
Your eyes flash and blink a life away
Touching the beginnings of hope
You cannot shelter and sway
You must grasp and climb the rope
And live the love you have learned each day
Do not be shy
But do not rush in blind
Smell the air and taste the sound
You may be surprised you find
The peace you seek this whole time
The cherished memories in your mind
So when I am gone
And years pass and pages turn
You may remember my name
Search out the site I lay
Smile and remember what you learned

"Unladen"

Come this way
You may
Recognize my plans
Same as the size
We put against the ride
Can you put words
And sing the promise in sync
With this unyielding truth
Love swirls
I've found the path
Head to her love furls
Unladen
Unknown
Perfection
Manifestation of love
Personification of living above
Wild he runs
To her who glows
He has looked from distance
Has evolved his dance
Displayed the romance
Never ending love sequence
Captured in thought
Captured in a tear
Forever comfort caught
Secured in loves vault

Book of Revelations

"This I Hold Dear"

Is this a day to smile
Mind wanders senile
Demanding attention
Recalling dimension
A God's distinct light
A single star
Admitting to night
Dark and oppressing
Eyes swollen shut
Demeanor depressing
Wondering about
Desperate for release into sunshine
A new world so divine
We've aroused a kingdom
Through arcane wisdom
The peace we seek
Is in the mind
We reach a peak
And scream our find
Locked together
A bond of souls
Latched with fire
Fates majestic hold

"Saint"

Step back and regress
Its prime time to reflect this mess
Remember what he taught
The lessons and thought
The battles I've fought
Dissect this dialect
Meaning meant to reflect
Truth and respect
The feelings he sends are sought
Behind billowing clouds of thought
You find
Avenues of truths
Meanings and enlightenments
Peaks of reflection
Heavens true suggestion
Open the doors to true redemption

"Futures Above"

Soul serenaded with the ambiguity
Of a future far from set in stone
But just this glimpse is worth
The hazy fog that burns my eyes
As I peak into the forbidden unknown
The suggestion from heaven
Is to fight nothing alone
Peaks, valleys and grown
Together, forever and prone
To loves laughing escapade
To twist of irony bending
Steeples made of steel
Gliding down this slide into what
Is exactly the essence I'd like to capture
This growing strength from distress
Holding out hope for the best
Never knowing what's in store for the rest
So through cryptic words of thought
Have I reached and tugged at your insight
Has my abstract art of words
Started to emancipate you from the funk
That has you certainly sinking deeper
And quicker in sand so far from where
You ought to be

"Cryptic Avenues"

My mantra is still going deep
Exploring depths my stylus seeps
Unto pages that reek of cryptic observation
And resonate smiles I want to keep
Illuminated minds are not
Without analytic exploration
Still deviant symptoms won't
Find a clear suggestion
Just a broader understanding
Of a choice well considered
Or a voice of Rose
Not completely withered
All mind, body and soul
Are poured into everything I have
Shelled for instants alone
Generating a concord of thoughts
Whether it's either here or there
Understanding has been cleared
To land anywhere
The fog has been lifted
To show the bright
And the gifted

"Selfless Again"

Death and denial
Wounds that never heal
Hate pushes the spiral
Until you cannot feel
Singed by fates hand
As I became a selfish man
I made angels cry
Felt the sting of God's demand
For 10 long years
I played with fears
Manipulated my peers
And laughed at their tears
I have come full circle
From the depths of being
Learned my lessons
And become a better being

"Would"

Given one more try
What would you change
Would you want to fly
Would you destroy the cage
Warped and strange
The mask of change
The eyes deranged
Across wind swept plains
Wonder in ever growing circles
Over hills and their eyes
Endless cycles
Filled with roundabout lies
I divided the sky
Evened the score
I will die
You can be sure

As I know
I will change
I will show
I can change
This desert wind
Covers up my marks
Blows away sin
And heals my tracks
The network of stars
Beacons crossed and tacked to
Interlaced and bizarre
But they beckon you
It's high time for change
High time to love again
I may be deranged
And I'll say again
I love you

"Only When I'm There"

A whispering lake dreamed
Streamed into a tethered silhouette
A fellow shady figure
Withered from unknown
Since I've grown
To a divination state
I pass through a guarded gate
See me free giving
But I've never shown
A talent grated
Into a harmonic tone
I trigger a vein
Left to be prone
In a position of stone
I'm left to dab into numb
A feeling from a gallon of rum
Just the sound
Of a pounding drum
In my brain
A ceiling so sane
Dance in our summer's rain
With your favorite dame
Without that ounce of pain
The dream of fame
And the purity of sanity

"Someplace New"

Warm weathers treat
Puts me on this new street
Watching as traffic passes
Through glasses of clarity
New faces grace me with sincerity
Ageless patience protect me with heavenly paces
Forward toward a bright but distant future
Places so few yet full of youth
The lies within the truth
Hidden traces of infected arrogance
Distance so far beyond deliverance
It's not so new when pens to paper
The revolving door that's been the steeple
The glue, the what we know
Is born each day we change
But it's always me covered in leaves
Hiding from the reality of what to believe
Because I want it to be different
I want it to be someplace new

"I Digress"

Success is a cobblestone path
Weaving on unconscious states
Though trunks have uprooted
Brick upon brick to stumble
The walk through a mind field of web
A mindful of taste deflates otherwise
Evil thoughts of disgrace
Inept rage swept under
The surf of ebb and flow pace
Deep understanding
Of what is required to digress
To happiness that is best shared
Days of the sun are
Inherently untamed
But every day there is light
Take me on this guided right
Free to intertwine with whomever
The heavens unite
And keep close those I chose
To envelope this life

"Ask Not"

Somewhere the candles stay bright
They fight and never flicker
Against the winds incessant bite
It's here, it's this find
Which has no ceiling
To the exploration of the mind
Been there and have come back
Bearing unspeakable gifts
That are impossible to define
Ask not their finds of enlightenment
Because yours will far differ
But rather ask the way to the door
And key to open it
From there you're on your own
You'll age, you'll weaken
You'll come back not speaking
You'll twist and turn
With sleepless nights you don't need
Yet when you sit back and regress
Digest all that you've been
You'll see the path you have walked
Was the righteous path indeed

"If You Had the Choice"

Another lifelong twist
To lead me to everlasting bliss
I can't compare
Your days straight
Your times fair
What else can tear at my heart
And dwindle my spirit
To experience early
Through thick
Never through thin
Or a path of perfect
To have never experienced
My days may be lasting
My story at an end
But these doors are open
The ways travelled
Your doors are locked
Leaving your maze expanding
The end always blocked
I'll be left still standing, head high
While you crumble crying
"My life has been a lie"

"The Man Demands"

Nagging thoughts that cross
The seventh layer of the seventh circle
Whispering suggestions to turn back
Afraid of when you become external
Trust in what you are and what you have
The dying light cannot save
Your soul from God's sight
Or your fears from judgment night
You can only attempt to suppress the cooker
To ensure the pressure subsides
The exposure that would divide
The inception of explosion
Stoking the flames of a burden unkempt
Left holding unsettling theories
As days of inflection fly by
Respecting the advent of a tortured mind
The man stands
Faces his mirrored reflection
The man demands
To be left in everlasting peace

"New Start"

Held before the light of the flame
I've bared my soul
Without spiral game
And without your control
I've been reverting sin
Swallowing the seeds of hate
I've been remodeling
My tomb like state
Hallow voices swirl
Mystic waves part
Her whispering call
Through open dark
I see the hand of fate

Reaching and touching
From beyond human state
To suggestive enticing
Entwined in the vast open
Of the unending never
We walk blind and broken
Hoping it's not forever
I know I must change
The circle must be complete
Spectrum of the deranged
We light and repeat
I will have come full circle
Back from dark the end of the vicious cycle
And a new start

"Circle Perfect"

Another taste of devotion
Rising these tides
And empowering the ocean
Flowering the minds
With these believing notions
Sending a chill
Of emotions
To change a flow
For all the Gods to show
All these mind altering potions
To the valley
And the shadow stream
To start this rally
To empower this dream
The chosen few will start anew

"So Small"

A formulated calculation
Set in every box
A cruel illusion
Displayed in a paradox
The worlds so far from ours
Surviving desperately
Against a sea of stars
Changing, evolving
Carrying a weight far greater
Then our religions could catch
Away at a distance
Destiny's erased
Fates replaced
A new beginning is placed
Time is new now faced
With an evolution of race
So open the book
That defies the mind
Steps you out of line
To journey in time

"Not Without Pain"

Controlling my devotion
To a gift far greater than many
Is a symbolic pool of emotion
Draining it on the field
And trying to refill it
With toxins that should be sealed
My rise to the top
Won't be without constant stops
More like walls that must crumble
For me to fumble with this further
Concentration and dedication
The C&D of my controlled devotion
And yet the symbolic pool
Is more like an ocean
Only growing with more emotion
And yet I won't fall
Standing tall I'll stall
But not at all utter a damming command
Because my retribution is at hand
From the gift I've wasted
Standing on solid land
When I could've risked it
And went swimming in the quick sand

"Striving for Perfection"

Personal and cultural confrontations
Dividing me both
Mentally and physically
On one side yaps
Only the ones that care
On the other side
Is someone I'm too scared to tell
I'll take you on this ride
Long and sweet
Dancing around the campfire
Until it's complete
It's a delicate tale
Of bravery in reflection
Starring me, a divorced mind
And constant inflection
From the context of life
Perceiving everything
With moral bias
About those actions
I don't believe I'm pious
I'm never contempt
With lives I see
Or the life I lead

"Poseidon's Reach"

The open deep and water fingers
Slide past in slow motion
The silence like listening to a new singer
Or learning a new emotion
Gliding over this land
Uncharted by man
Unspoiled by demand
Go deep to understand
Dive down deep
To this other realm
Let the ocean speak
Come out of your shell
Float on the currents
Marvel at the shapes
Forget topside events
Change starts from freedoms states
Follow the freedom
Forget the future
Let the mystery come
From the deep unknown

"Corner Stone"

In childhood I divulge
Down the only road I behold
Through challenges I wasn't exposed
And choices I never chose
Over fences I land
As years add up
Becoming the man
My parents brought up
Soon the times they changed
With a decision making hand
Now I understand
There is more than just
My feet in the sand
Through the births
Of any recognition
Now ignition past the sensation
Of a nothing incision
I want to make my mark
On the main line of the new edition
Knife the vein of mind and soul
And let drink to the new rendition
Let bleed
Till there's nothing left in it
Then Relive it

"Mystic Analysis"

Time slips and changes
Strange eyes alight
With yesterday's lost pages
Heathen gods drive red cars
Onward signs divide stars
Betrayed image
Of a virgins delight
Pacified religion
And shamanistic insight
I divine and pacified
I incline to rectify
The inquisitive sunrise
Lions roar in desert light
As flowers bloom at midnight
Stars blink SOS
As eyes watch from beyond
One twitch of cheek
As the smile turns
One preach of speech
Sets the souls to burn
Heightened analogy
Of the mystic analysis

"Mountaintop Crop"

Rolling right along
Without the serenity
Of the most beautiful song
Separating life from reality
Perfected and injected
Suggesting otherworldly looks
Neglected and dissected
All from untold and unread books
Mindful and colorful
Bashful and blue
We see sometime in tune
With what was reviewed
Held hand in hand
With God's love
We stand in quicksand
Wanting to be above
Now we see
From the mountaintop
Now we are we
Harvesting loves crop
I demand what I know
Show what I sow
Grow within what I hold

Book of Sorrow

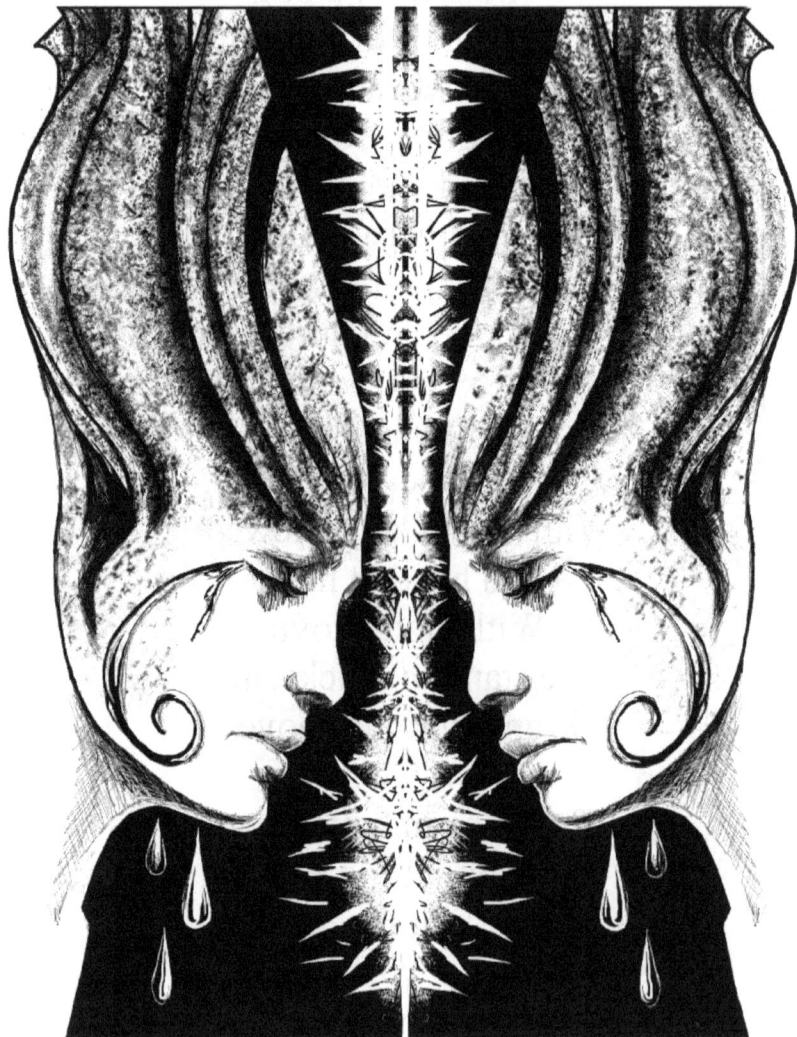

"Is This Worth Something"

The confusion
Magnified delusion
Condemned in detention
Life is at attention
A crack in the ice
Delivered pain
Understanding device
Damned and insane
Out in deep space
Agony on my face
I've lost my place
Discouraged and disgraced
Left to find
Secret corridors
Lost in my mind
Locked doors
Unknown rituals of flame and love
Circle hidden shadows
In the sky above
Fear awaited hours
Brow furrowed in thought
Eyes downcast distraught
Life little less than worthless
Is left alone
Soul worthless

"Investigation"

Operations built in the dark
Clandestine and shadowy
Your misinterpretation
Of my representation
Is telling you to eat me with lies
It's a conception
In retrospection
That you offer me complete knowledge
Of the wisdom that punctuated
In waves of discoloration
Instant overview
Of undercurrent formations
No perfection
Of exalted persons their execution
Just backward thinking systems
That map out the future
And the excursion into the realm
Of fugitive
Faced before the fall
Of your gravity pulling kingdom

"Got My Soul Singing"

A stepping stone in life's device
But the dawning days won't suffice
To heal the inside turmoil I feel
My mind unwinds like foil
Divines intervention
Couldn't even water my soil
I'm lost under a desert sun
With the snakes coiled for fun
Ready to snap and sink deep
As I seep away into nothing
My body quivers uncontrollably
Poison runs up my spine
Division bells ring wonders
As blood pours like wine
Hells doors awaits my soul
As I try to sing out
Pain waits with shouts
The devils rain ready to spout
A God's distinct light
Rushes to aid my fight
The end, yes my plight
But a savior saved me from the night

"Been There and Back"

I feel like I'm riding on borrowed time
Feel like my past is licking at my Achilles heel
I swallow and taste past grime
What will be the last thing I feel
I know the place I'll go
A small slice of heavens garden
Can't tell you, can't show
I'll sleep now with the denizens
Awake tomorrow without feeling again
Look skyward and smile
For alive now is the stain
Marked in life's shadow guile
The pain I bear
The weight I carry

"Life"

A tale of this brother's life
Pain ridden and riddled with strife
It could be me or him you or them
That lye strewn across life's broken highway
So don't look down upon
It may be you, you frown upon
Sometimes you see that chance
Where the kiss of bliss
Seems to be in your grasp
But it just dances away
All's you get is that split second glance
Then it's gone just as fast
But let's not fret
Tomorrow you'll fuck up again
For some more regret
You'll bitch and moan
Like in this poem
Until you piss your life away
So shit man
Might as well be stoned
Cause life sucks and
This is just one day

"Purgatory"

You can hear what you may
But I can't help what I say
I've been beaten and scared
Crucified by my mind
Left to die for my find
A lapse of time
When the wind blows
And the dimensions align
When my mind flows
I can't seem to bow down or win
A forever struggle drown in sin
The insanity sets in
I can't place it
Just left to face it
A death to this realm
Of the tortured and misfortuned
A stream of a thousand souls
Echoing pleases and calls
Bouncing off these prison walls
Locked and caged
Truly and forever dead

"Smoke and Dust Mist"

I grow tired of my sickness
Longing for the sweet ride home
Across the sands and seas
To my citadel of sanctuary
But the breaking point I've reached
They've all found their way in
Broken through my barriers and breached
Now it's a war inside and out
Death seems to be all about
I'll miss the moments of bliss
The times I flew high
Reaching the clouds in the sky
Yes, I'll miss all this
The rising sun
And the bright moon
In the dark of the night
The friends I have
And all those I'll never meet
So my end is near but always
I'll fear for my family forever
Yes, I'll miss all this
Miss the bliss
The cloudy smoke and dust mist

"Spin"

Moving ahead breathing feeling
Drowning in the breaths that are taken
Meant to give you life
Staring at the horizon
As the eyes grow colder and turn ice
With no feeling but regret and sorrow
A damned lost love remasked
To something not meant to be
Emptiness with no time and space fills
Overflow
Overgrow
Over so
Complacent in time
In a cycle
Round
Round
Round
Spin

"The Second Outcast"

Empty my thoughts and feelings
Unto a page of pain and rage
You, my brother
Has forsaken me
Not just from the distant past
Your backlash has beaten me black
From years of my mistakes
But I'm out of your wake
The stakes are too great
For me to drown in your hate
The more I give the more you take
Never mutual only for your sake
It's stabbing knives to know
We won't be old chilling with our wives
Drinking beers and grilling
Talking about life, sports
Or reminiscing the feeling
Of us being young
All the great times
And times that stung
Just simply brotherhood
That seems so empty now

"Changes"

Mystery is in the mind's eye
Digesting memories as time flies
A change in the everyday lift
Now having to sift through shit
To find that bliss centered gift
But hey, we'll see how the day plays
Maybe a challenge of solitude
Will organize my horrified dilutions of servitude
Maybe my vacant corners
Will perpetuate order
Developing me past my disorder
Yet again only time will tell
If I can climb out of this cell
Or with this new development
Sink deeper into hell

"Fading Pain"

The building blocks of life
Are pain and strife
Shallow whispers
Link the dead to hype
She has a silent hold
Strangling and stinging
We can never fold
Even though she is singing
We wrap ourselves in their breasts
Hiding from the truth
We are alone in every breath
Until we are removed
Sheared from love
We float in a lazy drift
So far above
We are below and ready to shift
We will shake free
From our prison of dirt
Turn the key and flee
To the western sea
We will build again
And rise from the ashes
The pain on the clock
Will fade in time

"Two Steps Behind"

I'm almost good enough
But still fall short daily
As I pick myself up from the rough tussle
I'm reminded I'm good enough rarely
I'm a master of devotion
But in the rough ocean
I poorly control my emotions
I'm a master of passion
But clashing often my dryness
Wilts even the sweetest fruit
I'm a master of laughter
Failing swiftly most times
To dodge the silence that erupts
After a painful moment of my clarity
But what can I do but try
And each day I progress forward steps
With sharp painful failures I regress
Loving every single second I'm a mess

"Lonesome Embrace"

Instances in time
Feelings of a past rise
Fate is showing signs
I circled back around in time
Cars race by
Noises of the needle
Internally I cry
An embrace to say goodbye
Images strengthen
An appointed heartache
Bathing in the past
A bittersweet taste
This meeting
That deepness
Clouded by time
Sparks seething
A bond
A bond

"Enough of Us"

Lips move but the sounds are muted
Expressions and gestures are implied
Gifted with the language that sees
Seven days of harrowing silence
Time ticking slowly by
The objective clearly marked
Words are the curse
The disease of expertise
Clear headed without the inclement squeeze
These schisms lingering for distances intense
Enlightening with a vibrant moral sense
Silver tongued extraordinary language of thee
Hands grasping fast around the lightening
The thunder rolling as an incessant plea for release
Dense fog hides the stencil of perfection
Extracted from a tomb a direction
Infectiously smiling away the shortcomings
But they police these streets
With electric sticks, brutality in a lick
The handpicked elites will compete to defeat
Any attempts at deceit

"Cracks"

There are so many cracks
That I'm tripping over doubt
Who has the hot wax
To seal the day in and day out
Free me from these constrictive obsessions
So I don't question my decisions
We are close to fulfillment
Close to a dreamed empire brought to life
I can't wait to be polished
But am afraid of what's next
I'm terrified to be without
Lacking a vision or purpose
Brashly floating freely
Crashing into those who mean no harm

"Cynically Pleasured"

Yours is a constricted view
Narrow headed in all that you do
Only if you opened your mind
And know that there are other things new
It's a constant headache
The way you twist and take
Feelings until they break
Its power you feed on
Like a commanding family don
Or a tyrant laughing cynically
At his kneeling pawn
Just fodder for the flames
Growing stronger each
Conquered minds your game
"Belittle his confidence
We'll take him and
Torture till he breaks"
It's painful to watch
It's hard to not
I wish you'd intervene
And make the hurt stop

"Stood up Again"

When the past is thought
I'm torn inside
Thinking of her last
Lusting ride
Then fury is familiar
Until it slips to present emotion
A painful potion
Poison more often than not
Trying to show love and devotion
Yet burning my chest
From the shot
Forgiveness comes easy to me
Almost giving in so she's free
To repeat the process
To her defiant glee
Not so accepting this time
I'll remind her to
Never commit this crime
Cause I don't deserve this
Showing true love
Then treated like piss
Stand up strong
Show her she's wrong

"Early Morning Dew"

My disease
A cancer remorse
From the first conception
Of the timely divorce
To the ashes within
Charcoaled from years
Of sex, smoke and sin
Dreams have been slated
To now a never reachable goal
Training for years
Fueled from dreams of "I made it"
Yet has the gilded man spoken
Wisps of smoke still rise above me
Breathless gasp for air that's nowhere
Yet how do I fair
Last, in a long race of despair
"I Can change" so abundant and true
With devotion long overdue
Propel a sunken vessel
To wind in sails red night view
Fields of dreams
Still lingering from
An overcast night
And the early morning dew

"Feeling Sieve"

What can I do
Simply serenade my
Sympathy unto you
This no longer empty page
Is half full
These feelings flow like fire
Pain embellishes the pages
Incriminates your hurt to ashes
As this book swallows them away
Your change is gonna come
Only in a nights rest
And rise of the sun
Pinhole pricks
Bleeds life from
An already drained life force
Now the demons stain your ink
As your hurt creases my pages
This instance of longing turned rage
Tip toes out of your pen
To this stage
I've already devoured
What you had to give
Move on my brother
I'm your feeling sieve

"Fall from Faith"

A pinch of pathetic pretenses
Leave me dismal and destined for what
Can't shut the thoughts
I'm caught in between the scenes
Yet all I want to do is let go
Show no feelings
No flow of conscious thought
One day I know one becoming
Of the devil inside
Shown outside gives me
Wings that melt made
Of wax to wither in the sun
No fun of flight the plight
Of falling of stalling
And dying
Towards the ground I go
In tow a baggage of buttons
Simply done and undone
Too many times
The crimes come forth
From birth, from brains
Chains link me to sink
Too heavy to fly
Too alive to die

"Doubt"

Gimme the grin
And the beautiful expression
Under this skin
The games and chains are wearing thin
I look at this weathered reflection
And cringe at the imperfections
Doubt leads to images untold
Unseen and so cold
Lack of trust
Busts up our sensuous lust
And you turn to me
And tell me not to fuss
Something out of nothing
I read deeper than I should
But the repercussions are evident
In lives and my minds clear evidence
So early in heaven
To be thought pure
Enclosed in scriptures
Turned pages to unlocked doors
Now the light fades to the night
The bite of the blue sky and waves
Dwindles to eerie dullness
I'm alone again in solitude
Alone again with just my poem

"Find your Way"

Screaming inside
Under this calm façade
The eyes tell all
Glassy with water welling and pooling
Drip, drip
A few drops fall
Yet more will surely follow
Wake up my dear aunt
Come back to us
Mind, body and soul
I miss your contagious laugh
Your never ending smile
More than me I worry
My blessed mother
My angelic grandmother
I feel that familiar sting
Of love and loss
Now only leave flowers for you
In the sweet sunshine
Wounded morning
Turn into gray
Find your way
My sweet aunt

"Heart Bled Dry"

Death a release
From the pain I am
No farewell speech
Or final goodbyes
Just what's written
As to say
I've ever even been
Look as to what I've done
All I've caused
The heartache of those inside
All for my cause
I'm selfish and self-indulgent
Does that make me ignorant
Or just another subject
Subjected to this prison
Shackled to my beliefs
And a heart bled dry

Book of Rebellion

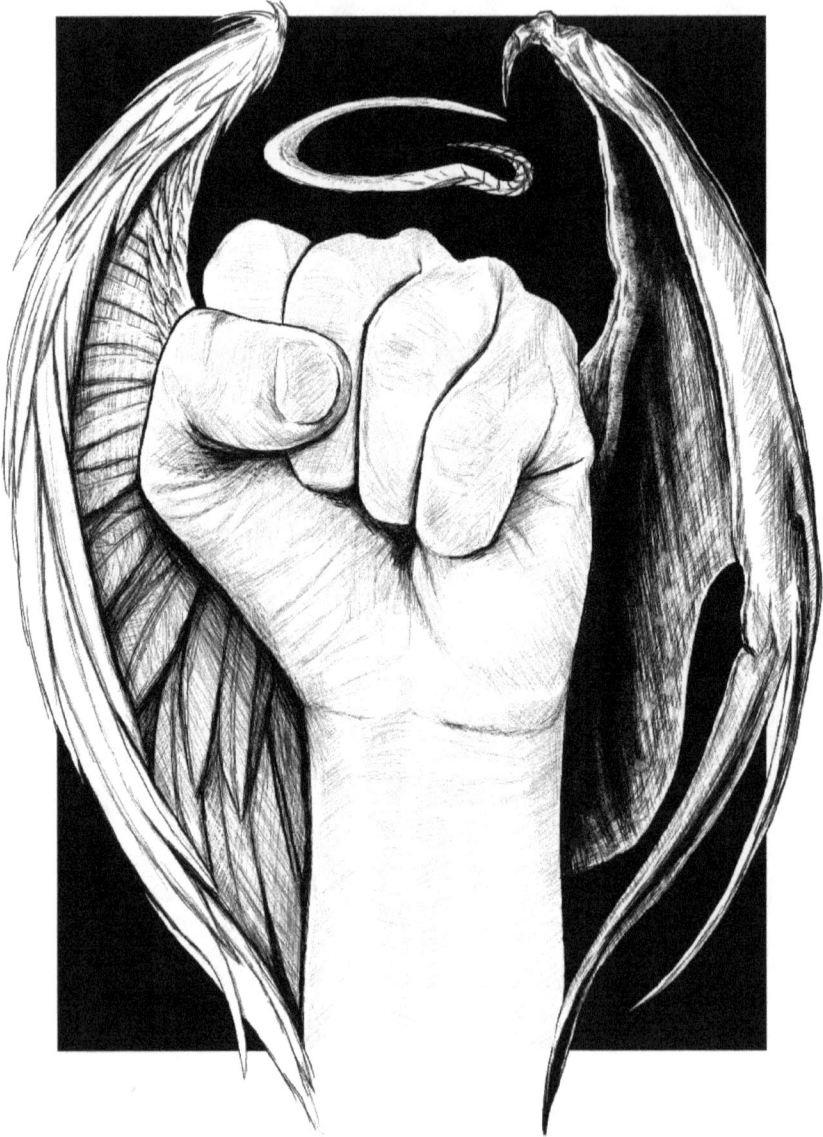

"The Unbreakable Reality Seem"

Keep rekindling the flame
Burns to flicker and dwindle
Of yesterday's down the drain
The swift descent of time
Of a life, a tiny grain
Spun my mind to define
The everyday of the dime
Lay me down slow
My furious fist and
Anarchist list
Drowned in the flow
This continual circular flow
Stains my existence
And pains my resistance
It's time to die in the stream
Like the trillion who died before their dream
Like them I have to realize
Death is the only end
To this unbreakable reality seem

"Be Free"

Let your dreams become reality
Keep your faith
Forget the insanity
Never give up
Never lay down
Stand awake and alive
Beside and behind the frown
Fuck all those people
Do they really matter
Do they line up outside your inner steeple
Forget their slave induced hate
Have away with that slimy feeling
Don't enter into their hell state
Become truth and start reeling
Roll forever, face to the wind
Eyes on the unknown ahead
Faith and belief in yourself
Until your bell rings

"These Machines"

It's an interesting web we weave
Our relations tangled in the breeze
The detentions of mine
Keeps me occupied in mind
These forgotten distractions
Lets fractions collide
Transform and divide
Cloudy decisions
Leaves me restless to lye
Detained in empty sleep
Then the tears turn to words
Of the fears of society
These leaves are my doors
Tied to the trunks
Far from the wars
The environments the core
You figure the financial figures
For February fall for failure
I see the selected visions drives
For a mission of corrected lives
Goodnight to the silent few
Saturday night
For the brotherhood crew
Far from society and you

"Tide of Vulgarity"

Smoke fills the room
And fragmented circles begin to grow
Masking the strange scent of the caged animal
Banging in the distance
The doubters will come, survey the scene
Make judgmental calls to governing people
In a faraway land
The animal eyes the show
Foam forms right before the release
You know the insane grows behind my eyes
And the pain seers at the soul
That is trying to escape
Blood boils at the contraption they set for us
Expecting us to fail flail and fall
Jumping through hoops set too high for the aspect
Of man is to jump and make his way into the
Afterlife as a winner
To feel a sense of accomplishment
I'm not right, my head is out in a different place
and I'm an insane man
Mimicking his way around
The rock of the unknown
Fuck you, fuck me
Ask not on a path of blame and there I'll stand

The statue you've known all along awaiting the
wrath you will set forth in a tide of vulgarity
And alone I'll still accept this as my own for it may
Be not but who else is there besides this fact of life
That set you onward a path of destructive taste
I may be beyond this eternity of social acceptance
And I will stop the teachings
Cause it's now mad ramblings of a child
Lost from his home for too long
I'm gonna die that's the facts jack, when it will be,
the dates set somewhere inside my head
And I've only scrapped at its surface so when I go
Will it be nicer for you, more peaceful
Or will you think upon the unknown swirling mass
Of gray matter in that bead behind that eye and say
Another pill
A thrill
A combination swill
Strap me down
Lock me up
Study this
My piss
Clean you'll see

"Stay"

Test my wave
Stay off the ride but see
It is what it isn't inside you
I'll be off they said
A bullet in the head
I'll be ok when I'm dead
Can't start over they said
So I'll stay here instead
Dropping skin
Flaking away like sin
Doesn't matter I said to myself
God to his mirror
Mirror God to myself
I softly drift away again
Back to this world my body lives in

"View"

Distilled vision and disrupted view
Interlocking heart quest
A condensed circle of blue
Should I move on to the next
Cryptic ideas of hate and disdain
Hacked to pieces without refrain
Logically insane
And soaking wet from the pain
I stand here in front of you
Naked and without shame
Do you see my ink etched bones
Entranced in their holy self
No sin now condones
The man free from the shelf

"Passive"

There is hope
Beyond the strain
Past the pain
Underneath the stain
Inside the mind
Savoring the state
Of being insane
It courses and flows
There for those
Who haven't fled the flood
No, it's for those who drank his blood
Gave no mercy killings
And kept on shelling
Inside my mind is alive
With rage and fury
Inside my hive
I've a direction of energy
I feel its buzzing
Hear the sound
Taste the sweet dripping
Over the ground
I just torched

"The Bitter End"

From deep inside
Strength flows
From body to spirit to mind
From my sister to brother
Our bond is blood
And it is forever
We have power
It thrives inside
Thrives in our bond
Encircles our lives
It makes us one
We together, rise together
We drive to the bitter end
Raging against the systems machine
We together, face together
We defeat the higher powers
We together, stand together
Until the final bell
Until the bitter end
The circle we created
Will circle forever
The power we have together
Will spiral forever
Until the bitter end

"Brother"

Have I been shown the truth
Has it been in my eyes
My entire youth
But see now I've
Seen the ties
All the lies
Within the lies
I've been illuminated
To this illuminati
I've been shown
Zach's just a kamikaze
A savior for the ignorant
A martyr to the ones that know
So as I sit and think
Steve's been the link
To a prophecy of ages
To a theory of reality
I'll pick up the pages
Where others left off
I'll free them
From the machine
Continue and keep raging
For you
For them
For everyone
Till the end

"Pathless Path"

Can you stand up to the truth
Spin a web around lies
Walk through the desert
Build a temple from ashes
A country from rubble
Wallow in spittle
Dive to the fathomless bottom
Walk past the great white wall
Forget everything
Be the hated object of earth
Set those free who hated you
Be fifty thousand different people
Bleed clear blood
Give your brain to one who looks like you
Defy the very ones who made you
All to be free

"What Do You Do"

Surrender the simple life
Because define
Momentary happiness
And eternal bliss
Riding that three foot wave
Might reward you with
Moments of happiness but
Gliding on that twenty three foot
Elemental deifier
Will put you on that list
To get a kiss from eternal bliss
You need to take those chances

Where at first glance
Seem like a desperate
And delusional trance
But really, at long look
Have the fuses to glue
Together your muses
And put you in a book
You have the power
To shower your enemies
With all your might
Or devour your sour pride
And offer that peace flower
So, what do you do

"Rebel Soul"

Resulting shock waves
Somersaulting past day
And bisecting passive plays
Instant instincts
Contorted eyes wide
Neurological condolences
And astral skies divide
Reunion and backtrack
Resolve your rights
Track your star flack
As it devolves your soul's defected sack
Your involvement in this war
Warrants special arrest
Your forthright thinking mark
Has touched life's test
Magnified and disconcerting
Solidified and disrespecting
Your souls reflective side

"Scribble"

Burn bright that iridescent light
While your smile flints the fires
That's burned our bridges
Now builds the foundation of empires
Made of skin to begin
This journey again within

Book of Insanity

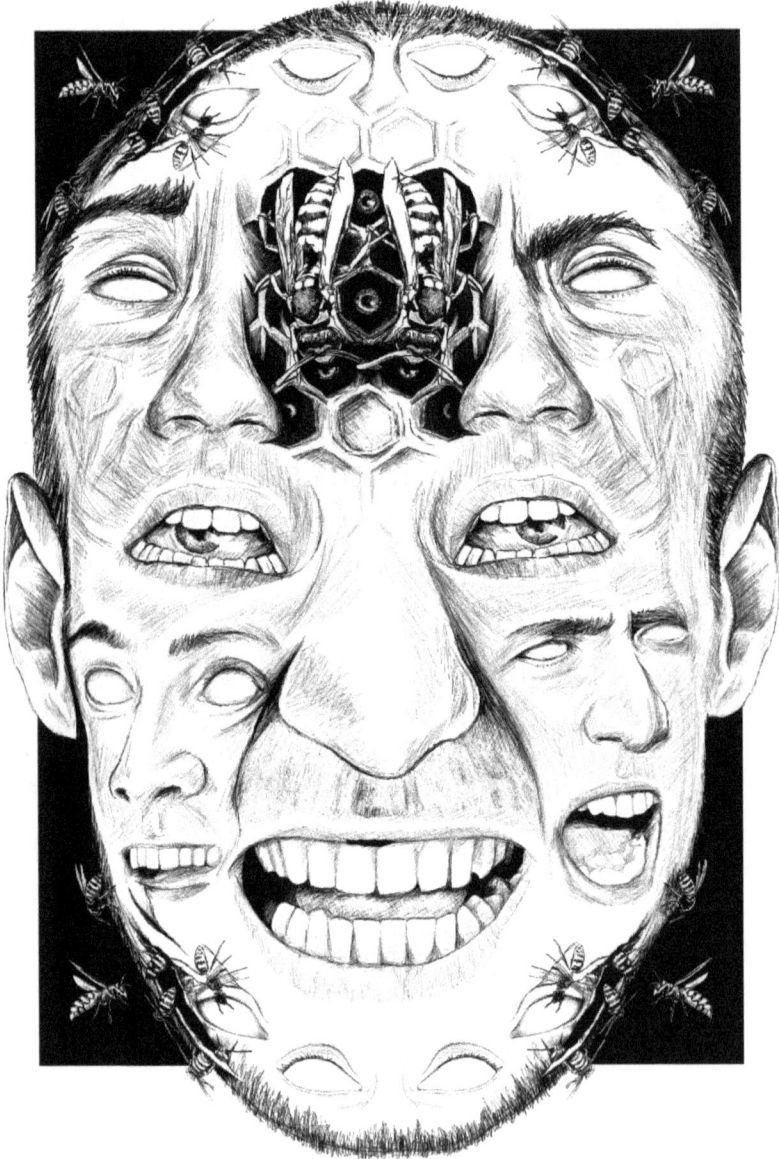

"Never to Awake"

I fall away to sleep
Giving this body the rest
But my mind the test
It races with insanity
To the fringes of reality
I've seen things
With indecipherable meanings
Dreaming of long lost friends
A lost love
And avenues of dead ends
Just a night full
Is enough to confuse the insightful
And turn even the tyrants
White and frightful
Although the streaks of sun shine
And the dream hours drag
Through circle of time
I continue to sleep
Enjoying the detentions of mine

"Total Satisfaction"

Surrounding people
Perked with pleasure
Inside this steeple
Performing arts and seizure
Faces scream
Plays the dream
Some it seams
On a medical rescue
Between the lies
Insanity greets
Smiles as he dies
Welcome to a higher seat
Uniform commentary
Cement in scenes
Protected chemistry
In a word of protected dreams
Wayward traveler
Passes perfection
Dies at the soul
To be together
Total satisfaction

"Just a Tiny Pin Prick"

I'm down with this sickness
That makes me leak with wickedness
They've no clue which way I'll go
All smiles or with bodies in tow
Cause I'll take you all down
I've no choice
I can't defy the voice from underground
Yet it's not a voice
More like a sound
That screeches at me to no end
I can't fend it off or block it out
The demons unleashed
Unwarranted and beseeched
They've taken my ores of freedom
Now I'm cast away with no way to reach them
Water logged thoughts
Squirming around infinity
To no source, no destination
Just to an end of meltdown
Complete on utter breakdown
Devastation on all fronts
From just a tiny pin prick

"Suggesting We End the Separation"

Wake the day away
Mindless thoughts
Deceased legends
And broken hearts
Leap through the spirals
Inner circles of faith
In the eyes of pain
Caught in a mirror flash
Faceless voices
Displacing knowledge
Weathered choices
Written within these pages
Convey to me
My date of release
So I can be
Without the diseased beast
Help carry the weight
The world hold
Lift my state
So I can behold

The majestic magic
Swirling in dream
Touching the tragic
Seeping through the seems
You are the maker of me
A strong devotee
To the lessons that be
Of the wisdom pasted down
To the knowledge I've learned
A man within this world of pain
From the eyes of fools I'm insane
Inside the turmoil
I turn
Look to you legends
To take personal responsibility
Of me in this dream reality
Make it easier, quicker
So I can come to serenity

"Detentions of Mine"

Dismantling my mind
Systematically and precise
A wonder of the beyond
Ignites the sights
Gut wrenching turnovers
Tornadoes of feeling
Steal a glance
Enter a trance
Mysteries are treasuries
Words for books
Written for God's children
Walking all a glaze
Eyes of boredom
Pay for entrance
To this, a place
A sparkling kingdom
Make this a place
Your eternal prison

Some earth Goddess
Come little princess
Sprinkle me mystic
Circle ritualistic
My mind is open
My eyes closed
My heart is open
My soul flows
Look deep into me
As I look to you
Look deep to see
The depths
Swirling time
Secretions of rhyme
Tripping mind
Detention of mine
Free me from reality
To serenity
Free me from reality
For eternity

"Hallway"

Deceit and tempered lies
Pain internal textured cries
Interwoven wax feelings
Revealing dancing figurines
Soft whispers of love and trust
Under views weathered beatings
Cutting through bloody dusk
Stepping out from fog shrouded nothings
Understanding flows after smoke clears
Repeating dormant fears
Masking pain with anger
And mixing blood with tears
Sweet swaying time slips away
Another day towards the grave
Yet the eyes stay bright and alive

The eyes
Until that day, the day I die
The world will continue to roll
The mark I lay onto the fold
Hallway walkway highway
Lined squared boxed angled play
To see through lying doorways
And pass unnoticed
From picture to picture
Scene to scene
Searching for the purity
That lies in the unity
Of seeing the you in God
And facing the God in you
In the mirror at the end of hall

"Reinvent"

Instant mist rising
Within a maelstrom of feeling
Constant steam blowing
From formless perspectives
I realize our demise
Lies inside
As eyes size
The times we've died
Your maze is mixed
With fucked up tricks
Messes with life
Causes our stress
Turns the knife
Killing what's left
Burning the genius of my mind
Learning to relearn the rhyme
Going back to the beginning of time
Searching dark recesses to find
A haunting nemesis
Without a face
Invading my perfect process
Leaves life with no recess
Us all truth we confess
To pass your constant test

"Fingertips"

Back to my roots
Flowers covered in soot
Finds through paths in time
Yellow precipitation
And a loss of rhyme
Distance is pain
Persistence drives like insane rain
The pictures I hold
Memories invade
Circling some unknown home
As I enter space to change
Fingertip ecstasy
And a runaway railroad train
Pulling them wrapped in chains
When will peace of mind arrive
How are we to notice it

"Everything"

The depths of my mind
Is doing reps to define
What truly matters
In a world full of sinners
And the essence of free thinkers
Wreaks havoc on me
Savage layers of my enemies
Not stopping their brutality
Until I'm on the brink of insanity
But it's been months since I've divulged
Into this book
My only drug that I behold
So where's been the release
Have I even been at peace
Is she making me who I want to be
Is she my muse or am I her puppet
Questions fill and spill onto this page
Yet answers are not as willing
As the ink is to come forth
So as I see…
These lines are jumbled with excess of thought
I have to continue to put forth
Or I'll explode with the burden of suppression

"All for Now"

I feel the darkness closing in
Feel the weight of our past sin
Closing around my brain
Feel like the insane is going to win
I'm being washed away
In two different directions
With more falling everyday
All without questions
I feel the noose
Around my neck
If it's my choice
Then why dissect
Cancel my pain
Reintroduce me to a higher comfort of living
Fuck the insane
And all the past sinning
Forget the game
I've faith in self
Wild crazy eyes will reign
And being tame is on the shelf
Embraced this insane
Run it over and through me
With the cold touch of ice cycles in summer
And slam one with the other side
I'll stare into the sun and sever a finger
All for now

"One Foot In"

Nesting in the necrophilia of life
The walking dead is nothing when the dead are
fucking with your spread of lies
We cry out on social media
We cry inside when shamed
We see the seeds we sowed long ago
When we placed blame
Now this hole is six feet deep
And we have no tears to weep
We await our time in line
Suggesting ways to die
Hearts are now our prisons
Minds the bars
Body the incisions we only see from afar

"Faceless Voices"

Beginning later after the light
Some head there before its right
Most ask what's beyond
Anyone's guess is as good as it gets
But for one to be dead already
We can see through the eyes of living
Can think what's been thought
You will be one who sees
Both sides of the spectrum
Entity as you believe
Like God as they seem
Finally that is the answer
But what is the spectrum
Not physical
Not mental
Architect of human kind
Creator of kind
Connector of earth

"Alien Mistress"

I am in the womb of an alien mistress
Who fucked Jim Morrison
Wanna play on my divided sky
Wanna get lost in my enchanted forest
Want me to lead you past yourself
Into the eyes of tomorrow
Slide on a twisted vine
As colors splash your face
Here, come, drink this wine
Spin the circles of the past
You are not really sleeping
Follow that mystic voice

You're not dreaming
But you have no choice
Come spin naked
This way the wind waves
Envelops misty eyed
This is the dream that saves
You can enter the valley
You can walk the path
You can dance safely
Without fear of death
Close your eyes my dear
I will take you softly
I will entrance your fear
Crystallize the captured tear

"Frog on a Log"

I know a frog on a log
Near a lake you can skate on
The frog croaks at the coat
The hoe stole from the goat
The frog swims with the things
That hymn to a distant ring
The story began as he swam in circles
Sometimes singing sometimes choking
The frog was old and told a fantastic story
Always bubbling about his story
But before he could score at the lakeside store
With the hoe who stole the goat's coat
He was hit in the head and was almost dead
The bells that rang as he sang
Were from inside his mind
As the frog returned to his log
Near a lake you can skate on
And as the bells rang
The song he sang inside his mind
He forgot the story of how the hoe stole the coat
From the goat
The day after there was
A wiser mind near the lakeside
He slithered and moved with a purpose
It's been a while since he dined
And he's never had a frog on a log

So the slithering snake moved through the reeds
On the side of the lake you can skate on
And he sees the frog on the log
Feeling dizzy from the bump on his mind
He makes plans to befriend the frog
So he makes up a story about a hoe whose coat
Was stolen by a goat
It was a fanciful tale woven with delight
From the lips of the slithering snake
That got close to the frog on the log
Near the lake you can skate on
And at the end of the day the slithering snake
Licked his lips as he finished the frog on the log
With the dizzy mind as the poor frog was distracted
By the tale of the goat who stole the coat from the
Hoe as she played with herself
Near the lake you can skate on
The snake sat in bloated delight in the reeds
Near the log the frog once was dizzy on
The steeds roamed free in the distance
Butterflies danced and weaved
The lake calm except for a slight breeze
But a movement caught a prehistoric eye
It was a bloated sign the slithering snake
Near the log the frog once sat on
And the eye contemplated
Darting from the steeds
In the distance to the slithering snake in the reeds

Near the log the frog once sat on
And a decision was made right then
In the lake you can skate on
Near the log the frog once sat on
The eye slowly disappeared
Not from fear but from anger
And hunger as he missed once the day before to eat
The goat that stole the coat
From the hoe that was playing with herself
With the swiftness of a goat stealing a coat
From a hoe the eye materialized
The eye became an alligator
That scared the steeds
Far from the reeds
Beside the log the frog once sat on
In the lake you can skate on
And with a sickening crash the slithering snake
Near the log the frog once sat on
In the lake you can skate on
Became the alligator with the prehistoric eyes
Lunch for the week since
He missed on the goat who
Stole the coat from the
Hoe that was playing with herself

About the Authors

R.S. Saint are brothers born and raised in New Jersey. They began writing at a very early age and have always used writing as a mechanism to map the minds musings. Whether their inspiration is women, conspiracies, pain, music or expanded consciousness, they seem to never be short of material and have been on a ride that has been nothing short of epic. Today, they each have day jobs and families but have found the time to publish a collection of their most cherished words.

www.ingramcontent.com/pod-product-compliance
Lightning Source LLC
Chambersburg PA
CBHW061749020426
42331CB00006B/1409